SPIRIT WARS

Johanna Michaelsen

HARVEST HOUSE PUBLISHERS
Eugene, Oregon 97402

Those names which, for any number of reasons, have been changed, are indicated by the use of an asterisk the first time they appear. All other names are the actual names of the persons mentioned, and permission has been obtained where deemed necessary.

Except where otherwise indicated, all Scripture quotations are taken from the New American Standard Bible, © 1960, 1962, 1963, 1968, 1971, 1972, 1973, 1975, 1977 by The Lockman Foundation. Used by permission.

SPIRIT WARS

Taken from **THE BEAUTIFUL SIDE OF EVIL**
Copyright © 1982 by Johanna Michaelsen
Published by Harvest House Publishers
Eugene, Oregon 97402

ISBN 0-89081-776-6

All rights reserved. No portion of this book may be reproduced in any form without the written permission of the Publisher.

Printed in the United States of America.

1

The Encounter

The tension was almost unbearable as we searched through the dark streets of Mexico City. We were lost. I peered at my watch in the light of a passing car. It was no use. We were too late to witness any of the operations scheduled for that night.

It probably didn't matter to Tom* whether we arrived at Pachita's on time. He had been there before to see her work. But Kim, my sister, was leaving Mexico the next day. This had been my last chance to make her understand.

"This is it! We're here!" Tom exclaimed as he jerked the car into a parking space in front of an old market. The pungent-sweet odor of rotting garbage in the gutter stung my nostrils as I stepped out of the car. Even a lifetime in Mexico had not accustomed me to that smell.

We walked across the dark street to a grimy white metal gate, which swung open even as Tom knocked. We stepped into a narrow courtyard crowded with people, some obviously wealthy, others clothed in rags, but all drawn together by a common bond of suffering which reached out into the unknown for the ray of hope and healing denied them by conventional medicine.

We made our way through the crowd toward

the entrance to the operating room. I was immediately overwhelmed by the smell in the room: musty dead roses and raw alcohol.

The focal point of the room was a large, tiered altar covered with dozens of jars and vases crowded with rotten roses. A picture of Christ on the cross and a large wooden crucifix stood surrounded by white candles. Next to the crucifix, in the center of the altar, was a bronze statue of *Cuauhtemoc*, the Aztec prince who had defiantly borne torture and death at the hands of Spanish *conquistadores*. At its feet lay a pair of surgical scissors and a rusty hunting knife.

My eyes turned to the right side of the room. There, on a cot, sat a wise old woman. A worn blanket was wrapped about her legs. She was smoking a cigarette as she talked to Tom. I watched as her stubby hands made frequent though tired gestures to emphasize a word or phrase.

I stepped forward and looked closer, unable at first to comprehend what I was seeing on those hands. They were covered to the wrist in dry, crusted blood.

I turned to look again at the altar. Waves of soft light now seemed to be coming from the image of the warrior and the crucifix beside it. "Lord God," I whispered, "thank You for this place. After all the years of terror You have now brought me into a temple of light. Let me serve You here, Lord."

My prayer was interrupted by the voice of a sleek young man. "Tell me, what are you feeling?"

he asked. With an effort I looked away from the glowing altar.

"I'm not sure," I answered softly, "I feel I'm in the presence of my God."

The young man nodded. "Then you must touch the statue of *Cuauhtemoc*!" he exclaimed.

I hesitated, them reached out my hand and with my fingertips lightly touched the image of the ancient Aztec warrior who was now Pachita's spirit guide, the one by whom the miracles of which I had heard spoken were performed. At the third touch a light shock ran through my fingers. Everything grew still and silent. I was enveloped in a deep velvet peace which wrapped itself around me like a mantle on the shoulders of a priest.

The man took me by the hand and led me to the old woman on the cot, "Pachita, you must talk with this girl!" The tired face turned to me and focused on my eyes, staring through me with a frightening intensity. No word was spoken for many seconds. Then a blood-crusted hand reached for one of mine and pulled me closer.

"You're very sensitive, very sensitive, aren't you?" she said softly. "Are you a medium?"

Her words startled me, and I hesitated.

"Well," she insisted, "are you a medium?"

"I . . . I'm not sure, Pachita," I answered. "Sometimes I think so."

"Well, my little one, you finish the studies in Mind Control you have begun with Tom and then return."

Then to herself she added, "We'll see. We'll see."

2

Great-Great Aunt Dixie

Aunt Dixie was Mama's grandfather's sister. Most of the family had been frightened of her and her strange powers. Yet there was a time when she was acclaimed by the crowned heads of Europe. Her picture appeared in newspapers of Europe and America for over 15 years.

The little Georgia magnet, as Dixie was known, could place her hands upon a chair, and without clenching it, raise it from the floor. A dozen men were unable to put that chair on the floor or break her hold without twisting and jerking it. She would lay her hands on a raised umbrella of steel frame, and the cover would suddenly rip off as though struck by lightning. In yet another test, she would, with one hand, raise a chair on which sat a large man, and hold it in her palm balanced on an egg.

Aunt Dixie was also known as a spiritualist and an effective trance medium. She died sometime in the 1920's—alone, forgotten, and a pauper.

It wasn't until June of 1975, two years after it was all over, that I learned of her prediction: Someone in the third generation—*my* generation—was to inherit her talent.

3

Mind Control

The colony I grew up in was located on the outskirts of Cuernavaca, 45 miles south of Mexico City. I was almost 12 years old when someone...something...moved into that home.

It happened late one night when Mama and Papa were away for a few hours. My sister, Kim, was asleep in her bed. I could see her from my room as I sat up reading. Suddenly, angry footsteps stormed down the hall...a door opened and slammed shut. Then another.

Kimmy sat up, startled, and rubbed her eyes. "Oh," she murmured sleepily, "Mommy and Daddy are home," and fell back to sleep. I got up and went into my parents' room to say goodnight...but there was no one there. The rooms were empty.

Suddenly I was afraid. I picked up my gun and walked into the living room. I felt a dead, clammy chill as if I had stepped suddenly into a giant icebox filled with dead flesh. The presence of something evil permeated the air and I began to shiver. The front door was standing wide open. Papa had locked it twice before he left ...but now it was standing open.... Yet there was no one in the house. I walked across the room and shut the door. Soft, low laughter began to echo in my head, a kind of laughter I had never heard before and which filled me with terror.

The being that moved into our home that night seemed to take a grim delight in frightening me. I was haunted by strange and morbid apparitions and voices for years to come, manifestations that increased and intensified during my college years.

"Hey, Johanna, listen to this," Father shouted up at me from his room where he was reading the newspaper, "and I quote: 'The Silva Mind Control Method. In 48 hours you can learn to use your mind to do everything you wish. You can learn to overcome depression, relieve insomnia, eliminate negative thinking, avoid irrational fears (Father's deep theater voice gave this last point special emphasis), relieve nervousness, develop ESP, and even gain peace of mind!' Sounds like something right up your alley, dear."

"What it sounds is bizarre," I said, coming into the room. "Probably some bunch of weirdos."

"More than likely," Dad agreed, "but at least it would give you something to do." He had a point there. I was depressed and lonely since my return to Mexico after graduation from college in the United States. There was no question that I needed something to keep me busy.

"They're having an introductory meeting to-night. Why don't you and Mother go check it out."

"On a Tuesday night in the rain?" I queried tentatively, not sure he was serious.

"So pretend it's Monday morning and take the umbrella," he retorted. We went.

The promises listed in the ad were confirmed and embellished at the introductory meeting by a confident-looking man in his mid-30's named Tom. He explained about the various brain-wave frequencies and assured us there was virtually nothing a controlled mind couldn't do, from developing genius potential to overcoming bad habits. We would even learn to heal diseases in much the same fashion as the famed psychic Edgar Cayce, the main difference being that we would learn to do it in a conscious state. All that was needed for the mental and spiritual evolution of man was this 48-hour training program.

Tom also told us about a wonderful old woman named Pachita and about the incredible operations she performed. The first time he met her, she had sliced open his knee and repaired an old football injury. The knee had not bothered him since. Mother and I signed up.

I gave myself joyously to the sessions, believing that Mind Control was my salvation indeed! On the third day of the course we learned to project our minds psychically into metals, leaves, and little animals ... but gently, very gently. Little pet birds had been found dead after careless psychic handling, we were told. "It all might, at this stage, appear to be imaginary to some of you," Tom pointed out, "but very real things are taking place on a different dimension. Trust me." I had long been aware of that other dimension and it had terrorized me for years. It was incredible to discover that there was a beautiful and positive side to psychic phenomena!

We went on to create our laboratory—a special room created in our minds which was to be our haven and refuge, our place for solving problems and relaxing. Mine looked like a shimmering amethyst and emerald cave.

Then, on the fourth day, we met our spirit guides. Silva Mind Control prefers the term "counselors." I knew immediately I wanted Jesus as my only counselor, but since we were told we had to have a female as well, I opted for Sarah Bernhardt. That night, however, both Sarah and Jesus manifested themselves as hideous werewolves. Fresh blood was smeared on their muzzles and matted hair, and yet a shimmering radiance still surrounded them. "Do not be afraid," I was told, as I watched the faces of Jesus and Sarah interchange with the horrible apparitions. "We only want to teach you that not everything that seems to be evil on the surface really is evil down beneath in its essence. When you truly understand this, our werewolf faces will be gone forever and you will ever see us as we really are." The message was clear: However evil they or any other apparition I might encounter might seem, it was not evil. It was just my lack of spiritual growth that made it appear so.

Within weeks of this, Sarah announced she was no longer to be my counselor and left. Seconds later, a small Mexican Indian woman materialized in my laboratory. Her eyes were deep amber in color, her face chiseled, but beautiful. She was dressed in a simple servant's garb. "You are to call me Mamacita (Little Mother)," she announced. "I have come to remind you of your coming role as servant. I will teach you humility and lead you into true wisdom." I knew with her arrival that the time had come for me to meet Pachita.

4

The Beautiful Side of Evil

The six days following my first meeting recounted earlier with Pachita were spent in deep mental and spiritual preparation. I sensed I was on the brink of my life's work and ultimate fulfillment in my search for God. I knew the years of fear were over; my spirit guides, Jesus and Mamacita, were with me, teaching me to overcome the lower spiritual entities. Now, during the many hours spent in meditation, waves of light and peace would flow over me, pushing away the darkness.

On Friday, July 27, 1971, the morning of the seventh day, I returned to see Pachita. I arrived around 11:30 in the morning. The courtyard was already crowded with people waiting to see *Hermanito Cuauhtemoc* (that is, "Little Brother," as the spirit who worked through Pachita was affectionately called).

Each person in line was instructed to have a fresh raw egg to present to Hermanito for the spiritual *limpia* (cleansing) which was performed on everyone during the morning consultation sessions. When my turn finally came, I stood before Hermanito, holding the egg in my hand. He placed both hands on my shoulders and, in a voice much deeper and gruffer than Pachita's own, commanded, *"A trabajar, m'hijita"* ("To work, my little daughter"). A strange shock ran through my body as his hands touched me.

"How do I begin, Hermanito?" I asked as he took the egg and began rubbing it briskly over my head and shoulders. He tossed the egg at the bucket that stood near him. It splattered on the floor. Hermanito nodded towards Memo, Pachita's oldest son, who was sitting on the cot.

"The son of my flesh will give you instructions." (Hermanito always spoke of Pachita in the third person calling her *"mi carne"* or "my flesh.")

Memo stepped outside with me as I left.

"What did Hermanito mean, Memo?" I asked him. Memo looked at me oddly.

"Hermanito is telling you that you will work as a full-trance medium—that you will one day heal as my mother does. You are to begin preparing immediately. Come back this Monday. Hermanito himself will tell you what you must do."

I returned as instructed the following Monday night. The sound of large raindrops was magnified as the rain pelted the tin roof of the altar room. A candle was lit and placed upon the altar. The single naked light bulb was switched off. Pachita put on Hermanito's satin robe and sat on the straight-back wooden chair in front of the altar. She told us to gather around her and pray. She closed her eyes, placed her hands straight and stiff on her spread knees, and began taking deep breaths. The atmosphere in the room seemed to thicken as a powerful unseen presence descended upon Pachita. Suddenly her body quivered violently. Her right hand raised in a sharp, straight-armed salute and a deeper, stronger voice than hers announced *"Estoy con ustedes, hermanos queridos"* ("I am with you, beloved brothers"). Pachita had vacated the shell of her body to make way for Hermanito.

Hermanito arose and directed a well-dressed woman named Rita to sit in the chair. Rita, obviously nervous, did so.

"Keep praying, my little ones," Hermanito said to us. "Only with God's will and help will we be able to heal this woman's eye." Chalio, a young engineer who frequently assisted Hermanito, stood behind Rita. He had cut large strips of cotton from the roll Rita's husband had brought. Smaller patches were placed in a small bowl and alcohol was poured over them, Hermanito's one concession to physical antiseptics.

Hermanito called me to his side. "Come, little daughter, you will help me." He instructed me to hold a large block of cotton under Rita's chin.

"Rita," Hermanito said, "I want you to sit very still now. Keep your eyes open and looking up at the ceiling. Do you understand me, little one?"

"Is it going to hurt me, Hermanito?" she asked, her voice quivering as she spoke.

"No, little one, you are even now being anesthetized," Hermanito said reassuringly. He took the new bottle of alcohol I was holding, opened it, and poured it directly into her eye. I gasped, expecting the woman to cry out, but she just sat there. Then Hermanito sprinkled some of the balsam on the eye.

"Very well, little one, now hand me the cotton you have there." As I handed him the smaller cotton strips, he formed a square leaving the eye exposed in the center. Then he asked for the scissors and the old knife that lay on the altar. Hermanito took the scissors and raised them in a salute toward the altar as he began a prayer in *Nahuatl*, the ancient Aztec language. As he prayed, I saw that the area where we stood, and especially around Rita's head, became much brighter than the rest of the room, as though a soft spotlight were shining down on us. I could see clearly. I was to witness this phenomenon at each of the several hundred operations in which I assisted in the coming months.

"Pray to God, little ones!" Hermanito pushed one point of the scissors into Rita's eye and began to cut. A pale reddish-white liquid trickled into a piece of cotton that fell off her face and dropped onto her chest. I caught it and replaced it, my face only inches from her eye.

"Do you feel pain, little one?" he asked her.

"No, Hermanito," Rita answered. Her head began to turn as she spoke.

"Keep your eyes open—*open*." He began peeling a thin opaque scum off the center of the eye. It broke. He placed the first piece on the cotton I held out; then he gently lifted off the second part of the tissue and handed it to me. Again he poured alcohol into the eye, then placed a clean pad of cotton over it.

When the job of bandaging was done, he instructed two men to wrap Rita in a sheet and carry her across the courtyard to rest in the house.

The entire procedure had taken perhaps 15 minutes. A week later I learned that Rita's operation at the hospital had been cancelled. The doctors were astonished at the total disappearance of the cataract.

Rita's operation was the first operation I had ever seen Hermanito perform. It was on that night that Hermanito gave me instructions and meditations for becoming a full-trance medium, even as Pachita was. She had been working with Hermanito for 46 years at that point. "Hermanito has performed marvelous healings through me," she later told me, "but I don't know for how much longer. I am old and tired. My sons have refused my mantle. They are too busy with their own things to sacrifice themselves in this work. It will fall to you, little one, for you are gifted and willing. I will teach you all I know."

I made the trip across the mountains into Mexico City at least once or twice a week, sometimes more, to be with Pachita and to assist during the consultations and operations. I saw incredible things—things which defy belief.

The second time I assisted Hermanito was during an operation in which he opened up an old man's back and replaced several badly damaged vertebrae with healthy ones taken from a fresh corpse at the morgue.

"This poor man," Hermanito said. "No wonder he has been in pain." After replacing the vertebrae, Hermanito noticed a small tumor at the base of the man's spine.

Again the knife went into the wound. Suddenly an incredible stench filled the room. Instinctively I lifted my hand up to my face, but Hermanito grabbed it and placed it back inside the wound. "Hold the tissue taut, little daughter. I must remove this tumor. It is cancerous." He cut something loose just above my fingers and pulled out a round, stringy mass of flesh about the size of a golf ball, which he then wrapped in cotton to be disposed of. Hermanito took a large piece of cotton which I handed him and swept the bloody cotton aside, passing his hand over the wound. It closed as he did so.

The pain the man had been feeling before the operation was gone and there was new, fresh color in his face. He was smiling and talking. Yes, he had felt Hermanito working inside his back; he had felt pain, but he was fine now.

I lay in bed that night thinking about the things I had seen. Was it possible that it had all been a trick? Had it all been sleight of hand and a fraud? Had I been hypnotized? The replacement of the vertebrae was medically impossible. But my face was only inches from the wound. And I had a clear view of Pachita's hands, which were open, fingers spread. Nothing was palmed in them. At no time did she pull anything out from under her tunic. And I had felt the warm blood pulse over my hands. My hands were *in* the wound—blood was smeared to my wrists from it. But what she did was impossible!

That's right—for any human doctor. But the being working through Pachita was not human. He was supernatural—he was beyond the realm of physical laws as we know them, and so the effect and works which he performed were also supernatural and not bound by conventional rules.

The spirits are right then, I thought to myself. My sister, Kim, was wrong. This work of Pachita's was not satanic. How could it be? Was there not a crucifix on the altar and a picture of Jesus? I had seen nuns and priests there, sprinkling holy water throughout the room and reciting the rosary. All glory was given to "My Father and Lord"; we were constantly told to elevate our thoughts to God and to say the Lord's Prayer. Besides, what purpose would Satan have in healing and doing good works? No, there was no question in my mind that what Pachita did found its ultimate source in God. I was therefore determined I should work there to learn and serve as best I could. I praised God again and again for having led me there.

5

Exodus

By September 1972 I had been working with Pachita for over 14 months. I had washed the blood of over 200 operations from my hands. I had seen everything from the removal of brain tumors to the replacement of vertebrae and lung transplants. I had seen things materialize and removed from the human body during *dano* (curse) operations which further defied belief and logical explanation: handfuls of live worms scooped from one woman's stomach; a white arrowhead from another's heart; and yards of hideously rotten, bloody, mud-covered rags which I helped Hermanito unravel from a woman's abdomen.

Despite all I had learned in the last year, I was not a full-trance medium as Hermanito had said I would be. I was not growing as I should, as I knew Hermanito had expected me to. He had said nothing to me about my failure, but I could sense his disappointment and I felt vaguely ashamed and uneasy.

But there were other things that troubled me as well. I was finding that some cures Hermanito performed were only temporary. I also couldn't understand why Hermanito treated Pachita so cruelly—never allowing her any new or pretty clothes, and refusing to treat her when she was sick, which was often now. And her family was falling apart around her. Over the months, what peace I had perceived there deteriorated in the presence of almost constant tension and bickering among her children.

Things had become too hectic. The vision was no longer clear as it had seemed when I first arrived. I needed to get away for a while, to spend time alone where I could commune with God and find my way again.

For six weeks I wandered about England. Eventually I found my way to Florence, Italy, to see my sister, who had been living there for several months since her graduation from college that summer. Quite frankly, I had mixed emotions about visiting her. As a committed Christian, Kim was certain all my pet activities, namely yoga (I had been teaching hatha yoga and learning raja yoga for about a year), Mind Control, and psychic surgery, were "of the devil," and said so. I was equally assured of the fact that she, on the other hand, was a narrow-minded, bigoted, Bible-thumping evangelical, who wouldn't know a genuine miracle from God if it ran her down in the street. After all, I had spent much of my life terrorized by evil beings. I *knew* what their source was. But now, through meditation, Pachita, and my counselors, I was seeing wonderful things, miraculous operations, hope restored, evil spirits cast out. Granted, there were a few discrepancies I couldn't explain, but nevertheless Satan couldn't heal, could he?

I had been in Florence with Kim for only a few days when, not altogether unexpectedly, the general thread of this conversation was soon picked up and we were off again. This time, however, Kim's tactics took a slightly different bent. She asked questions—questions which now began echoing some of my own hidden doubts.

"You say you can tell the difference between good and evil spirits, but how can you be sure your senses haven't been deceived?" "Yes, Pachita performs amazing operations, but how do you know for sure her source of power is God?" "You say you believe in Jesus—but which one?" "How do you know the Jesus you see in your laboratory is the Jesus of the Bible?" "How do you know demons are truly being cast out. Is it possible they are playacting?"

I had to admit, if only to myself, I didn't really know. The only argument I could fall back on was my experience—my feelings and perceptions. Yes, I had read and studied the masters, Edgar Cayce, Allan Kardec. I could give eloquent explanations when asked about reincarnation, karma and cosmic consciousness, and astral planes and psychic manifestations. But when it came right down to it, I knew there was no solid, truly objective way of testing the source behind them, and that troubled me. How *could* I be sure the source was God? I had no absolutes against which to compare my experience.

For the first time I sat still and quiet under the gentle but insistent onslaught of Kim's questions. Finally she stopped and took my hand. "Look, Johanna, why don't you go to L'Abri in Switzerland for a few days? Os Guinness is a counselor there—he knows a lot about these things. Maybe he can help make all this clearer to you."

I looked up sharply. L'Abri! I knew that L'Abri was a place of Christian study and ministry founded by Francis and Edith Schaeffer. It was the last place in the world I wanted to go.

"Don't look so distressed," Kim laughed. "I'm not asking you to move in permanently; just go for a couple of days and talk to Os. It can't hurt to listen. Besides, your train goes near the place on your way back to England anyway."

I took a deep breath. "All right. I'll go. Who knows? Maybe there *is* something for me there."

To my relief the image I had of dozens of fire-and-brimstoners trying to convert me on my arrival at L'Abri never materialized. After several days of relatively peaceful anonymity, I decided to talk to Os and Sheila Bird (the counselor with whom Kim had suggested I spend time before seeing Os).

Sunday morning, after chapel, I had someone point "Birdie" out to me. She was a small woman probably in her 40's. I watched Birdie's face as she spoke with a young girl. Her eyes were stern, but kind. As I moved closer, Birdie glanced over at me and stopped in mid-sentence. "You must be Kim's sister!" she exclaimed. I nodded.

"Kim called several days ago. Os and I have been expecting you. Why don't you come by my chalet after lunch today for a visit?"

When I arrived at her chalet, Birdie ushered me into a tiny, cozy room and finally, after much gentle coaxing, had me talking about the beings and manifestations that filled my life.

She was silent for several minutes after I had finished.

"Well, Johanna, I can certainly see why you believe as you do, but something about what Pachita is doing makes me uncomfortable. Let's not talk about it just now, though. First I'd like you to spend the next day or so reading the Gospel of John and the first epistle of John. It will help lay a foundation for our next meeting."

It seemed a reasonable request. I had read 1 John and the Gospels several times in the past, but the words never had the same impact on me that they had now. The Jesus I was encountering on the pages of that Bible was not only alive and real, but was filled with awesome power and majesty. A mere spoken word of healing or deliverance was sufficient to bring it about. His claim to unique incarnate deity was unmistakable, despite what I still believed about it. Verse after verse asserted that apart from Him there was no forgiveness of sin.

I was shaken and confused by the time I finished the last verse in the Gospel of John. If what I had just read was true, then everything I believed about karma and the way to unity with God was wrong. It couldn't be both ways. The claims made by Jesus were too exclusive. And if I was wrong about what I believed about Jesus, then maybe I was wrong about the rest as well.

Despite a well-rehearsed, serene exterior, I was in turmoil by the time I arrived at Os Guinness' home to talk with him about the eastern aspects of my belief system. Part of me wanted desperately to know the truth, another part of me still wanted to shut down and ignore the whole business. Os spoke to me about the irreconcilable dichotomy between the Eastern and biblical view of God, salvation, and Jesus. While I had always believed that Hinduism and Christianity were fully compatible (Swami Vivekenanda had said, "We accept all religions as true"), Os emphasized that, far from compatible, the two philosophies were radically opposed to one another in their basic concepts of God, reality, morality, and personality. He pointed out that although several gurus taught that the teachings of "the Blessed Lord Jesus Christ" dovetailed perfectly with Hinduism, their claim lacked scholastic integrity. These gurus, Os continued, lifted phrases such as "The Kingdom of Heaven is within you" out of context and blatantly ignored other less pliable statements such as "I am the way, and the truth, and the life; no one comes to the Father, but by me" (John 14:6 RSV). This point especially caught my attention as this had been one of the sayings of Jesus with which I myself had long struggled and had sought to explain away. It was too intolerant a statement, too narrow-minded to possibly be anything other than a misinterpretation or mistranslation of the Bible. Yet the first epistle and Gospel of John were filled with such statements:

> And the witness is this, that God has given us eternal life, and this life is in His Son. He who has the Son has the life; he who does not have the Son of God does not have the life (1 John 5:11,12 NASB).

> I said therefore to you, that you shall die in your sins; for unless you believe that I am He you shall die in your sins (John 8:24 NASB).

Os summarized his discussion by saying: "It is quite plain that, if treated fairly on its own premises, Christianity excludes the full truth and final validity of other religions. If Christianity is true, Hinduism cannot be true in the sense it claims. Even though on the surface it appears that Hinduism is more tolerant, both finally demand an ultimate choice."[1]

Intellectually, Os' discussion made sense to me. Spiritually, however, I couldn't accept it. I felt torn between two powerful, relentless forces. The pressure finally drove me to my knees.

I again challenged God to once and for all show me the truth. Was Jesus the greatest avatar, the way-shower; or perhaps the greatest creation of Father God; or was He God uniquely incarnate in human flesh who died to take my sin, as the Gospel of John and Os and Birdie and Kim claimed? Was Pachita working in the power of God or was her source satanic?

"If You can, God, show me now. I'm willing to give up Pachita and yoga and all the rest if I'm wrong. But if not, then I'm putting all this nonsense aside and going on with it at Pachita's. Oh God, let me see the truth!" I had no idea how literally God would answer that prayer.

❀　　❀　　❀

The night of November 15, 1972 was damp and cold as I walked alone on the slippery path to Birdie's chalet. A dense, black fog was forming all around, blotting out the path. Within seconds I could see nothing. The dark mist was swirling, alive, filled with the presence of something more monstrous that anything I had ever before encountered. Voices began whispering, hissing incoherent words and laughter in my right ear. An ice-cold breath touched the back of my neck under my hair.

"Hermanito, help me!" I gasped. The voices shrieked in hideous laughter.

"We're going to kill you!"

I panicked and broke into a run. Something like a giant fist slammed into my back between my shoulders. I pitched forward in the thick darkness and instinctively reached out to break my fall. My fingers found the branch of a small bush and clung to it. I tried to scream out "Jesus!" but an iron hand closed upon my throat, choking off the word. All I could do was scream in my mind "Jesus, Jesus, help me!"

"He can't help you," the voices shrieked. "He can't help you!"

But then suddenly the grip around my throat loosened—the blackness lifted. I could again see the light of Birdie's chalet at the end of the path.

Birdie's eyes widened a little as I burst into the room. "What on earth is the matter with you!" she exclaimed.

"I don't know, Birdie," I said, still shaking, "but I'm terrified."

Birdie hurried me into her little prayer room and closed the door. She took my hands in hers and began praying. I tried to focus on her words, but suddenly they sounded so far away. I felt dizzy. My eyes opened. The room seemed to have been taken up in a giant slow-motion whirlwind, spinning slowly round and around. The sound of voices began to build again. I turned my head toward the dark window on my left and froze. Outside I could see the faces of countless demons, contorted, twisted in indescribable rage.

"What is it, Johanna?" Birdie's voice was muffled, as though it were coming across a vast distance.

"Can't you see them, Birdie?" I gasped. "Can't you see their faces?"

"No," I heard her voice say, "but I know One who can. Satan, in the Name of Jesus Christ of Nazareth, I command you to be gone! I forbid your presence here. I claim the protection of the blood of Jesus upon us. Go where Jesus sends you!"

Instantly the faces vanished. The room stopped spinning and was filled with a peace beyond all my understanding. They were gone.

I knew what had happened was a direct answer to my prayer. God had literally let me see the source behind my practices. Murderous demonic rage had been the spirit's reaction to my potential decision to accept Jesus Christ of Nazareth *as He is*, rather than as I had come to think He should be. The difference had been subtle, but vast nonetheless. There were still so many things I didn't understand, but I knew beyond any doubt that I had been wrong about Jesus.

Two days later—Friday, November 17, 1972— at 10 A.M. Os and Birdie supported me in prayer as I renounced my involvement with the occult and committed myself to Jesus Christ as my Lord and Savior. I would never again face the darkness alone.

1. Os Guinness, *The Dust of Death* (Downers Grove, IL: InterVarsity Press, 1973), p.50.

6

Test the Spirits

I have not written this story as an exercise in narcissistic morbidity. Writing the account of my life—reliving those days of darkness—has been one of the most difficult things I have ever done. Nor have I written my story to glorify the deeds of darkness. I have shared my story because of the times in which we live.

Those of you who are—or have been—in the occult, and are seeking a way out of the darkness, or those of you who have friends or loved ones still under bondage, will understand the relevance of my story. In these last two chapters of this booklet I share some of the basic principles I have learned from many years of hard study and personal experience concerning the discernment of false prophets and healers, and the means of freedom from occultic bondage. I pray these chapters will be of help and encouragement to you.

Demonic Wonders

To assert that demons do not work miracles, that no medium can indeed receive manifestations of a supernatural nature, one must wreak awful havoc with the testimony of both the Old and New Testaments. From Genesis to Revelation God speaks of a powerful being whom He calls Satan and continually warns us against him and his awesome, malevolent, seductive power.

We see the magicians of Pharaoh reproducing the signs God gave through Moses, doing "the same with their secret arts," turning their staffs to serpents, turning the waters of Egypt to blood, causing frogs to cover the land. These are impressive tricks for "mere frauds." But there came a point where they could *not* counterfeit God's plague of lice (despite the fact that I always thought lice were from the pit of hell and Satan's own). Their failure forced them to admit, "This is the finger of God" (Exodus 8:19).

In Deuteronomy 13 we are warned concerning "a prophet or a dreamer of dreams" who arises among the people and "gives you a sign or a wonder, and the sign or the wonder *comes true* concerning which he spoke to you, saying 'Let us go after other gods (whom you have not known) and let us serve them,' you shall not listen to the words of that prophet or that dreamer of dreams; for the Lord your God is testing you . . ." (Deuteronomy 13:1-3).

These terms, the Hebrew *aoth*, which means "signs," and *moteth*, which is the word for "wonders," translated by Old Testament scholars in the Septuagint around 250 B.C., are the same words used by Jesus in Matthew 24:24: "For false Christs and false prophets will arise and will show great *signs* and *wonders.* . . ." The word *aoth* translates as the Greek *semeion* (signs), and the word *moteth* is *teras* (wonders). These are precisely the same terms used to describe the miracles of Jesus in the Gospel accounts. Hal Lindsey tracked these terms down for me. He concludes that whether in reference to demonic miracles or those from the hand of God, these words can in no way be taken to imply fake signs or wonders such as those produced by the skilled magicians of today.

Revelation 16:14 speaks of the "spirits of demons, performing signs," and the Antichrist himself, when he is revealed, will perform "great signs, so that he even makes fire come down out of heaven to the earth in the presence of men" (Revelation 13:13).

Demonic miracles *do* take place. The question that must always be asked is not only *Did a genuine miracle occur?* but also *What is the source behind it?*

We have been commanded to test the spirits (1 John 4:1). Very well. But just exactly how do we do that? How can we be certain a healing or a miracle is from God? How can we be sure our own gifts are from the Lord? The existence of a counterfeit presupposes the existence of an original. I believe that the gifts of the Holy Spirit, including miracles, healings, tongues, words of knowledge are still valid today.

God has not offered us His supernatural gifts and power only to leave us permanently contorted by the terror that it may all be a demonic counterfeit. Many pastors have felt a reluctance to discuss counterfeits at all for fear of that very thing. As a result, many of us are left in ignorance of Satan's schemes and techniques and therefore vulnerable to them.

The Lord in His Word gives us several basic tests to help us distinguish the true prophets from the false ones. This task is not always a simple one, for a false prophet will rarely oblige us by admitting to it up front. Therefore, it is important to discern on the basis of *all* these tests, not just one or two.

The Tests

1. *What does a prophet (or healer) believe about Jesus?*

Does he cling to Jesus Christ of Nazareth as God the Son, second Person of the Trinity, God incarnate in human flesh; the God-Man who died upon the cross in our place for the forgiveness of our sins; the One born of a virgin whose physical resurrection from the dead proclaimed His victory over sin, death, and Satan? Does that person believe it is "by grace you have been saved through faith; and that not of yourselves, it is the gift of God; not as a result of works, that no one should boast" (Ephesians 2:8)? Or have they, through subtle redefinition, come to accept "another Jesus," "another spirit," "another gospel"? (2 Corinthians 11:3,4)

In Deuteronomy 13:1-5 the Lord states clearly that even if that prophet or dreamer of dreams works genuine miracles, if he in any way seeks to lead you into trusting in another god, you are not to listen to him "for the Lord your God is testing you to find out if you love the Lord your God with all your heart and with all your soul."

2. *A prophet must be 100 percent accurate 100 percent of the time.*

> And you may say in your heart, "How shall we know the word which the Lord has not spoken?" When a prophet speaks in the name of the Lord, if the thing does not come about or come true, that is the thing which the Lord has not spoken. The prophet has spoken it presumptuously; you shall not be afraid of him (Deuteronomy 18:21,22).

The prophets of today, as perhaps you've noticed, have a tendency toward inaccuracy. Even Jeane Dixon's failings are staggering, never mind the rest of the channelers and psychics! It should be obvious that if God were the source of their prophecies He could have gotten it right the first time.

3. *If a miracle or sign or prophecy or healing is performed by an occultist, or by means of occultic techniques, it is not from God. It is counterfeit.*

God made his position on the occult remarkably clear in Deuteronomy 18:9-14 where He lists the full gamut of occult categories, from superstition and channeling to child sacrifice, and flatly labels them *detestable* (the King James Version uses the word *abominable*). In case we missed it the first time around, He repeats it three times (in verse 9 and twice in verse 12). It is not because these occultists were "stealing away business," but because God knows the demonic source behind these practices and does not want His people to be contaminated by them (Leviticus 19:31).

God spoke through His prophets by inspiration and dreams and visions, not through occultic techniques. But false prophets receive dreams and visions as well and may not use actual techniques of divination, such as crystal balls or tarot cards or Ouija boards or astrology, or tea leaf reading, etc.[1]

That is why *all* these tests must be applied. No single test, in and of itself, is sufficient. A false prophet or wonder-worker might pass one or two of these tests yet still be speaking lies and producing counterfeits.

4. *The test of the fruit of life must also be applied.*

What often characterizes false prophets is a rebellious, unrepentant spirit, but not always. Frequently their *lives*, their moral standards, are totally above reproach. Matthew 7:15-23 is a key passage here. The Lord warns us against the false prophets "who come to you in sheep's clothing, but inwardly are ravenous wolves" (verse 15). How will we spot them? "You will know them by their fruits" (verse 16). The Lord then goes to great lengths to explain the basics of spiritual agriculture, reemphasizing that a good tree cannot produce bad fruit and vice versa. However, most people never read past the verse that again says "so then you will know them by their fruits" (verse 20).

> Not everyone who says to Me, "Lord, Lord," will enter the kingdom of heaven,

but he who does the will of My Father, who is in heaven. Many will say to Me on that day, "Lord, Lord, did we not prophesy in Your name, and in Your name cast out demons, and in Your name perform many miracles?" And then I will declare to them, "I never knew you; *depart from Me, you who practice lawlessness*" (verses 21-23).

It was not enough that these who used the name of the Lord prophesied or cast out demons or even performed many miracles.

They said therefore to Him, "What shall we do, that we may work the works of God?" Jesus answered and said to them, "This is the work of God, that you believe in Him whom He has sent" (John 6:28,29; see also 1 John 3:23).

It is the "fruit of doctrine" that gives eternal value to the "fruit of life." Without a personal relationship with Jesus as Lord and Savior, the fruit of life is ultimately meaningless.

5. *The final test is that of our subjective inner witness.*[2]

It is through the clear, clean Word that God Himself reveals His Son—our Cornerstone. It is through the Word that He equips us. But ultimately we come before our God on a deeply intimate and personal level in which we feel His love and tender compassion for us; in which we experience the joy and deep serenity of His presence in our lives. The supreme goal of our existence is to love and know . . . experience . . . Him.

When we walk in fellowship with our Lord, as we come to know Him, His Holy Spirit bears witness within us concerning these things. But where we have grieved His Holy Spirit through sin and disobedience, this inner witness becomes warped and distorted and we no longer see or understand. Our inner witness may no longer be accurate.

The Lord said, "If any man is willing to do His will, he shall know of the teaching, whether it is of God, or whether I speak from Myself" (John 7:17). If we truly want to know the truth and are willing to be obedient to it, God will make it evident within us.

Sadly, too many of us insist our inner witness is the first and most important criterion. I myself once said, "How can you tell me the work at Pachita's is demonic! I have felt the presence of the evil beings; I have experienced the good; I can tell the difference." No, I couldn't. And neither can anyone else who has cut himself off from testing his beliefs and experiences against the inerrant Word of God. Experience is, by definition, subjective and totally open to manipulation by those who know how to "tickle our ears" (2 Timothy 4:2-4) into rejecting God's truth in exchange for myths and doctrines of demons (1 Timothy 4:1).

---

1. Hobart E. Freeman, *An Introduction to the Old Testament Prophets* (Chicago: Moody Press, 1968), p. 110.
2. Ibid.

7

The Means of Freedom

It may be that some of you who are reading these words do not believe in Jesus as your Lord and Savior. Some of you may have read this far out of sheer curiosity, but some of you may have read this because you are seeking release from demonic bondage.

No Freedom Apart from Jesus

Understand then, before anything else, that apart from Jesus there is no hope for you. "There is salvation in no one else; for there is no other name under heaven that has been given among men, by which we must be saved" (Acts 4:12 KJV).

Unless you are prepared to commit your life, your body, mind, and spirit to His Lordship, you will never find the peace and freedom that you seek. "Come to Me, all who are weary and heavy laden, and I will give you rest" (Matthew 11:28), Jesus says to you. His yoke is easy. His load is light.

Satan will yoke you to his lies. He will lure you as an angel of light that he may ultimately burden you with terror and destruction. But the awesome witness of the Scriptures is that "The Son of God appeared for this purpose, that He might *destroy the work of the devil*" (1 John 3:8).

It is He who has "disarmed the rulers and authorities," for "He made a public display of them, having triumphed over them through Him" (Colossians 2:15). It is Jesus who through death upon a cross rendered "*powerless* him who had the power of death, that is, the devil" (Hebrews 2:14).

For All Time

Those who stand in Jesus need never fear the loss of their salvation. "*All* that the Father gives Me shall come to Me; and the one who comes to Me I will certainly not cast out . . . of *all* that He has given Me *I lose nothing*, but raise it up on the last day" (John 6:37,39).

For Him to lose a single one of us who has come to Him in faith would make Him a liar, for He has said *all* who come shall be raised up with Him. We cannot somehow undo what Christ has done at the cross. "For by one offering He has perfected *for all time* those who are sanctified" (Hebrews 10:14). Because He took our sins upon Himself and paid the penalty for them, God the Father is no longer hostile toward us; *all* our transgressions have been forgiven, for the decrees against us were *paid in full* at the cross (Colossians 2:13,14).

> I, even I, am the one who wipes out your transgressions for My own sake; and I will not remember your sins (Isaiah 43:25).

All who are in Him are *now* seated with Him (Ephesians 2:6) at the throne of God. Our *position* there is secure, for Jesus Himself said:

> My sheep hear My voice, and I know them, and they follow Me; and I give eternal life to them; and they shall *never* perish, and *no one* shall snatch them out of My hand. My Father, who has given them to Me, is greater than all; and no one is able to snatch them out of the Father's hand (John 10:27-29).

Not even *we* can take ourselves out of the Father's hand once we are His.

Satan's Goal

Since, therefore, our souls are forever secure, what is it that Satan is seeking to steal away from us who are in Christ?

C.S. Lewis said it: "The next best thing to a damned soul is a sterile Christian."

Satan would rob us of our witness, making us into stumbling blocks to those who are perishing; he would rob us of our peace and of our joy; he would rob us of our freedom; he would rob us of our fellowship with God. This is why we are *constantly* exhorted to walk according to the light (1 John 1:6,7); to be on the alert (1 Peter 5:8); to "put on the full armor of God that [we] may be able to stand firm against the schemes of the devil" (Ephesians 6:11).

Blatant immorality, the deeds of the flesh in Galatians 5:19-21, pride and rebellion, participation in the things which God has called abomination, all give Satan the toehold he seeks in our lives in one way or another. Occult activities make us especially vulnerable to demonic oppression. This is why it is important to "shut the door" which we may have opened in our lives to his influence.

Writing a "Stop" Payment

Every sin connected with sorcery constitutes, in a very real sense, a pact with the devil.[1] It gives him the legal right to bind and oppress that person (Exodus 20:3-5), *regardless* of how that door was opened. Perhaps you were charmed by a medium or a healer as a child; perhaps you inherited the demonic burden through your family line, even as I did. It may be that someone with mediumistic gifts laid hands on you, thereby transferring his powers to you to some degree. Perhaps you only "played around" with a Ouija board, or with aura manipulation or with astrology. The fact that you may have only viewed these things as a joke doesn't make a bit of difference to Satan. Once you trespass into his territory, you may well become fair game and the focus of demons.

Regardless of how it happened, there is only one way to shut the door: through coming to Jesus in confession and renunciation.

To confess our sins means simply to acknowledge them before God; that is, to agree with Him that what we have done was wrong and in violation of His will. It is important that this confession of one under occult oppression take place, if possible, in the presence of a mature believer or a Christian counselor for two reasons:

1. *To bring into the light the secret, hidden things.* The occultists in Ephesus who turned to the Lord "kept coming, confessing and disclosing their practices" (Acts 19:18), renouncing the hidden things (2 Corinthians 4:2). It is especially important that every known resentment and sin be confessed, not only those connected with occultism, so that any foothold Satan may seek to keep in our lives is removed. This confession cannot be forced from the person. If it is not voluntary—from the heart—it is worthless.[2]

2. *To lift you up in prayer* as you legally revoke Satan's claim in your life. The devil will not be pleased and may, in some cases of severe oppression, put up a struggle before releasing his hold.

Spend some time before you pray considering the things you will want to confess. In some cases it may be helpful even to make a list of these things, asking God to show you what it is you need to bring before Him.

Destroy Occult Objects

It is also *most* important that you collect every book or object related to occultism in your possession and destroy them. Don't just throw them in a garbage can where your neighbors can get at them. Make sure the objects are smashed, burned, or ripped beyond repair. These things often act as crystallization points for demons. Get rid of them (Acts 19:19; Deuteronomy 7:25,26).

Prayer of Renunciation

The following prayer of confession and renunciation can be used, but the words themselves are not somehow sacred. It is the intent and attitude of the heart which matters before God.

> Almighty God, in the Name of Your Son Jesus, I renounce all the works of the devil.
>
> I confess and renounce all my occultic practices and sins as an abomination before You (list them here).
>
> I renounce any occult influences from my forefathers and I ask, Lord God, that You now break any hold Satan may have had in my life because of them.
>
> I pray that any evil power or ability I may possess, or which has oppressed or possessed me, be completely destroyed and removed from me, for I want no gift that isn't Yours.
>
> I commit myself, my body, my mind, my personality, my emotions, my whole being, to the Lord Jesus Christ to be my Savior and my Lord.

Just as our salvation is by grace, through faith, "and that not of yourselves; it is the gift of God;

not as a result of works . . ." (Ephesians 2:8), so it is with our deliverance from demonic bondage. It is not based on our performance or merit. It is not dependent on our feelings. Regardless of your emotional state at this point, if you have come before God with an open heart in this confession, you have the assurance of the Word of God that "He is faithful and righteous to forgive us our sins and to cleanse us from all unrighteousness" (1 John 1:9). The door has now been officially closed, but don't think that means the battle is over. On the contrary, in many ways it's just beginning. Therefore, put on the full armor of God!

The Blood of the Lamb

The end days are upon us. False Christs and false prophets and false miracles will continue to increase as the second coming of the Messiah draws nearer.

But however subtle the deceit, however furious the warfare, the believer who clings in obedience and in faith to the Messiah need NEVER retreat in fear at the onslaught of the demons or their counterfeits. The one who in obedience to God's command puts the spirits to the test cannot long be deceived.

It is not enough, though, not to be deceived. We must become active warriors in these evil days, knowing that *in Him* we are *more* than conquerors (Romans 8:37). It is the demons who flee in terror before the one who understands the victory and the power in the shed blood of the Lamb. It is that blood which has shattered Satan's grasp upon us.

> And I heard a loud voice in heaven, saying, "Now the salvation, and the power, and the kingdom of our God and the authority of His Christ have come, for the accuser of our brethren has been thrown down, who accuses them before our God day and night. And they overcame him because of the blood of the Lamb and because of the word of their testimony, and they did not love their life even to death" (Revelation 12:10,11).

This is the greatest weapon God has given to His people: the protection of the blood of the Lamb, that blood which has cleansed us from all sin. Because you are in Him, you have the authority to plead that covering as protection in the battle against the devil.

Commanding Satan

Because of that shed blood, we can dare come against the devil, commanding him to flee before the name of Jesus. "I command you in the Name of Jesus Christ to come out of her!" Paul ordered the spirit of divination who possessed the slave girl. Luke 10:17 records the joy of 70 disciples who exulted in the fact that "even the demons are subject to us in Your Name!"

We can dare command the devil *only* because of our position in Christ. We have no power in and of ourselves, so beware of getting haughty with the demons, ordering them into the pit—for even Michael the archangel "when he disputed with the devil and argued about the body of Moses did not dare pronounce against him a railing judgment, but said, 'The Lord rebuke you' " (Jude 9).

Some men "revile the things which they do not understand" (Jude 10).

But in the victory of Christ, as we stand under the authority and protection of His blood, as we are filled—that is, controlled by His Holy Spirit—we can command:

> Satan, in the Name of Jesus Christ I bind you and rebuke you. I command you to depart and go where Jesus sends you.
>
> I remind you I am a child of the Living God; you have no authority over me.

Then ask the Lord's covering:

> Father, I plead the covering and protection of Your blood. Fill me and shield me about with Your Holy Spirit.

These words are not a magic formula to be churned out as an automatic mantra. Nor are they a prayer to Satan. They are, rather, a word of command issued by an embattled child who understands the fierceness of spiritual warfare and the authority granted him by our victorious General.

Those who have come out of occultic backgrounds may find themselves resorting to this command many, many times throughout the day, as I myself did. Satan does not let go easily. He knows he has lost the battle for the soul, but will nonetheless rage against the person who renounces occultism. Do not be afraid. Fear is perhaps the greatest weapon Satan can throw at a believer. But God's "perfect love casts out all fear." When you feel Satan come against you, know you have the authority—the command—to resist him. He *will* flee from you (James 4:7).

God's Armor

Make use of the *full* armor of God. No warrior goes into battle with only the parts of his equipment that happen to appeal to him.

Because our struggle is not only against flesh and blood, but against the world forces of this darkness, against the spiritual forces of wickedness in heavenly places, *therefore* take up the full armor of God. Unless we are girded with the belt of His truth, our armor will not hold together; unless we have put on the breastplate of righteousness of Christ, our hearts can be pierced through with pride and self-righteousness; unless our feet have the sturdy cleated shoes of the gospel of peace, we can be thrown off balance by the first wind of doctrine that hits us; unless we take up the shield of faith, Satan's flaming missiles of doubt and temptation will lodge deep in our flesh and burn us. The helmet of our salvation guards our minds; the sword of the Spirit, which is the living Word of God, we alternately use to defend ourselves and thrust forward "piercing as far as the division of soul and spirit" (Hebrews 4:12).

How is this armor appropriated? How do we put on what God has said we need to stand firm against the schemes of the devil? It is upon our knees in prayer that this is done (Ephesians 6:18).

Never underestimate the power of prayer and worship in the battle against Satan! The Lord abides in the praises of His people. It is as we praise and worship the living God that the darkness cringes back, for it cannot stand the presence of the Light.

There is a beautiful side of evil—deceptive, subtle, adorned with all manner of spiritual refinements, but no less from the pit of hell than that which is blatantly demonic.

But to us who have believed it is said: "You are from God, little children, and have overcome them; because greater is He who is in you than he who is in the world" (1 John 4:4).

May He grant us the grace and wisdom in these last days to walk as children of the Light.

---

1. Kurt E.Koch, *Occult Bondage and Deliverance* (Kegel Publications, 1968), p. 100.

*This booklet has been
excerpted from Johanna Michaelsen's
245,000-copy bestseller—
dealing with the occult and psychic phenomena*

The Beautiful Side of Evil

Are all miracles from God, or is there a beautiful side of evil? The blind see, the deaf hear, and the lame walk. Is God always behind such miracles, or can there be another source?

This is a true account of a young woman who, while in search of spiritual truth, became a personal assistant to a psychic surgeon in Mexico for 14 months. Then, in answer to her prayers, God revealed the true source behind the miraculous healings she witnessed. Lifting the veil of deception, He allowed her to see the evil behind the outward appearance of beauty and holiness. Johanna Michaelsen reveals how this deadly deception is not isolated to her unusual experience but rather is invading our everyday lives, even our churches.

*Available at
Christian bookstores everywhere*

"JOHANNA MICHAELSEN is uniquely qualified to write about this subject. I have never met a person who has so sincerely and wholeheartedly explored this area. . . . I have had ample opportunity to verify the facts of her life fully. I testify that this amazing story is absolutely true. . . ."

—Hal Lindsey